RollerCoaster

by
Marion Perrotta

Order this book online at www.trafford.com
or email orders@trafford.com

Most Trafford titles are also available at major online book retailers.

Printed in Victoria, BC, Canada.

ISBN: 978-1-4269-1663-2

*Our mission is to efficiently provide the world's finest, most comprehensive book publishing
service, enabling every author to experience success. To find out how to publish your book, your
way, and have it available worldwide, visit us online at www.trafford.com*

Trafford rev. 10/28/09

www.trafford.com

North America & international
toll-free: 1 888 232 4444 (USA & Canada)
phone: 250 383 6864 ✦ fax: 812 355 4082

Index

Foreword

Growing up in a small northern town in Alberta Canada, and although I was surrounded by a large and loving family, I always felt the need to escape.

Not from the ones that doted on me, but rather an escape to my "self."

Writing poetry became my refuge and my passion.

As 40 years flew by and the chapters of my life unfolded, I collected and saved all of my written reflections. These are a reminder of where I have been, what I have learned and most importantly who I have become.

RollerCoaster is a recollection, through laughter and tears, of the ups and downs of life and its lessons.

Something in these verses may strike a familiar chord because I believe that life is really just a rollercoaster ride and we are all on it.

Acknowledgements

Special thanks to my husband Tony for all his love and
support.

Thank you to my daughter Lana Jazo for "That day in
Paris"

Eternal gratitude to my Lord and Savior....

Without Him, I am nothing.

To my family, thank you for loving me.

Dedicated to Auntie Clarice

...my intuition in the garden of roses

RollerCoaster

The tracks are calling out my name.

The silver cars are waiting

to tie me in and take me on

to a life I am creating.

I'm holding on at every height.

The wind is my companion.

I float and fly,

I dive and soar,

like an eagle in a canyon.

The twists, the turns, the rise and fall,

at speed

I've never traveled.

Joy and fear wash over me.

I watch as life unravels.

What fun! What fear! What fury!

Oh I am in my glory.

From where I'm perched atop the track

I now can tell my story.

Looking up and looking back

onto the track

over my shoulder,

I realize

this crazy ride

has served to make me bolder.

Love and fear ride hand in hand.

The two I comprehend,

as I go rolling down the track

on a rollercoaster

that never ends.

Big Brother

The years between us
The father we share
The mothers who brought us
to believe love was rare.

We had each other
and didn't forsake
the special bond
that siblings will make.

When I was lost and needed to find
a rock I could cling to…
a word that was kind…
Your strength came shining like morning sun
and showed me there was no need to run.

Under your wing

and your watchful eye,

I came to believe in you

and I.

For me there truly is no other

that could take the place

of my Big Brother.

Coco

I remember the day I met you
under your mother's kitchen table.

We were very young…maybe 4
You were wearing a dishtowel as a cape
and you told me your name was Mighty Mouse.

I told you my name was Marion.
You put your cape on me
and called me princess.

I've loved you ever since.

Daddy's Hands

The day I came into this world
though I could not understand,
the first thing I remember was
being held in my Daddy's hands.

His hands proudly held me.
I felt his heart beat fast.
I rested deep into his arms
I met my Daddy at last.

His lips came down upon my face.
A tear slid down his cheek.
I knew the love he felt for me
before I was able to speak.

Time has passed and I've grown up...
Now I am able to stand,
but I'll never forget the love I felt
held in my fathers hands.

First Love

He came to me young and alert

with gleaming eyes and a glowing smile.

His voice was tender so clear and pert.

I treasured his presence

all the while.

I need to make friends with my mirror first

where I must find the approval I thirst.

So what if I still look like a child?

I'm 13 and my heart is beating crazy wild.

All I want is to see him smile

and maybe dance with me awhile.

I've spent times alone and others with friends,

but the best times are spent with a boy named Glen.

I Love You Baby

I'm 16 and I'm carrying a child.

Where can I run where can I hide?

I love you little baby growing inside.

My body is changing and my thoughts are scattered.

I'm frightened but I love you

and that's all that matters.

I didn't mean to make you so soon,

but it looks like I'll be a mommy by June.

I love you baby… never forget

and nobody knows about this yet.

End of Innocence

Little princess of the dawn,
you live in a world of newborn dreams.

The moment you were taken from your warm, soft,
safe and quiet
and brought into this cold, hard and
unpredictable world,
I felt your anguish as I watched you flay
your tiny arms towards the sky
and cried for the peace you left behind.

Forgive me…
I'm young…
And tomorrow is a scary word.

Moonlight Lullaby

Freeze dried light
turns your body into night.
It will all turn out alright
in freeze dried light.

Little princess of the day
haven't heard a word I say.
It will all turn out ok
in freeze dried light.

Little princess of the night
have no fear have no fright.
You are such a pretty sight
in freeze dried light.

Vancouver Island

It's been too long since I've seen the sun
come out of the empty sky.
Only mist and fog and dreary days
from December to July.

The weeks and months go swimming by.
There's nothing to mark a change.
What day is it?
What time is it?
Doesn't matter cause it's all the same.

The ducks and geese,
the grass and trees,
are waiting from hour to hour.
I hear them call for rain to fall.
They're grateful for the shower.

Grey and black umbrellas

dot the street below.

Guess I should be happy.

At least it isn't snow.

Lintlaw

You know.

You've known it all along.

I…yes I… have to

make it all on my own.

I tried to see the light in you,

but you turned

and said to me that we're thru.

What can I do

to make it

all up to you?

You know I would if I could.

It doesn't matter

what they say about it now.

It never did.

Teenagers

Why does it take a major jolt today

to shake a minor detail

into those who are stuck in tomorrow.

High above the clouds they are

so oblivious...so blind

to what is happening right in front of them.

Don't be in such a hurry to chase tomorrow

when today needs to be handled now.

It's not possible to make the destination

before the journey.

Trust me and I will show you how.

So

slow down

or you'll fall down

and life will be a total

let down.

This I know to be true.

Fifteen

Love is not easy on the young

when hearts are just an open book.

Today you're sad with a heart filled with tears.

It's just a rehearsal for the coming years.

You'll learn that love may bring you pain,

but oh the lessons you will gain!

Take your time and think it through.

Heartache is not done with you.

Remember

Do as I say

Not as I do

Gerard's with my Girls

It's so warm in here and I don't mean

the weather.

Ambience abounding, like coming home to family.

Where the heart is.

Words of wisdom come pouring from your mind.

You know how it is.

Such a place is this

with men in balloons over colored hills.

Bring on the virgin coladas.

A toast to my babies

..that I love so much.

Mama's in the Kitchen

Gather round my apron strings
and bring your smiley faces.
Mama's gonna cook some things
from distant far away places.

We'll start with something made in France…
Sexy, sweet and delicate.
A glass of wine to make us dance
while we simmer the Crepe Suzette.

Now we'll venture way down south…
to the land of hot jalapenos.
A Salsa that fires in our mouth
and sizzles down to our toes.

We mustn't forget the Roman food
where basil and cheese are the motto…
For this we must be in the mood
for Linguine and Risotto.

What say we venture further north

to Poland, Czech and Russia.

We'll stir up Krupnik and Cold Beet Borsht

And dine like the King of Prussia.

Now we'll wander to the Isle of Crete...

the land of eggplant and lamb.

Where Spinach Pie and Souvlaki

are the best in all the land.

You say you'd like to taste some Thai...

I must say it's my favorite!

The Lemon Grass and Curry Pie

are calling for us to savor it.

Holiday Children

Christmas twinkles of pale misty blue.

Here I sit thinking how much I miss you.

Holiday children with faces that shine.

I can't help but wonder "Oh God where are mine?"

Are they at home or are they away?

Please keep them safe both night and day.

Fill them with joy at this special season,

knowing they are loved for so many reasons.

And come Christmas morn and come Christmas night,

may someone who's near them please hold them tight.

And make sure that their dreams and wishes come true.

Merry Christmas my darlings

from your mom who loves you.

Love Don't Come Easy

I say I want it…you say you've got it.

But I don't see it and I don't feel it.

You say you need it… I say I'll give it.

But you won't see it and you won't feel it.

Baby the first one to go is the last one to know.

Feeling…not believing.

Caring … never sharing.

Opposite attraction…fatalist distraction.

Trust in the good times.

Pray in the bad times.

To want, to need, to give, to see.

Mama said

"Love don't come Easy"

Maui No Ka Oi

Take me to the place...

the only place my heart is free.

Cast me in the sun,

let my spirit be.

It's there that I left my heart

beating on the wind.

And when I dream…I see it there.

Crazy as it seems

your spell has got me bound.

Timeless dreams, my heart's the only sound.

And when the waves come rushing through,

the winds will take my thoughts of you

back to where they start...

beating in my heart.

Pony Dream

There comes a pony in a dream
to sweep you up and ride away.
You say you're not prepared to go
for fear that you'll have nothing left to show
the ones that watched you fall apart
and mended up your broken heart.

The happy horses, the joyous jockeys
all standing at the edge of time.
And there you are with your little star
prancing at your place in line .

Your pony rears and you cling onto
whatever you can muster.
You both fall away
to a brand new day
into a starry cluster.

You ride along into the light.

The stardust leads your way.

Your pony never tires

of running night and day.

You ask yourself what place is this

so far away from home?

A voice comes to you,

a chill runs through you

and you are not alone.

Far in the distance I hear

a voice that interrupts..

and my reverie

is telling me..

"It's time now to WAKE UP"

Stepping Out

Holy frijole, today's my birthday

and I'm stepping out in my Sunday best.

With my darling wrapped around my arm,

let's put the Tequila to the test!

I'll make a wish that fills the day

with laughter and song and dance.

Come with me baby, let's get away.

I need some drink and romance.

Spin me round in circles till my feet are off the floor.

Let's hoot and holler, scream and shout.

Pass that bottle…gimme some more.

You know what this is all about

so you better look out

cause I'm stepping out.

I'm stepping out…

I'm stepping out…

Whoops I fell down…

Confusion

It scares me

and it haunts me.

It calls to me

then it runs from me.

And it returns to me

and laughs at me.

It cries for me

and it lies to me.

It loves me and despises me.

It plays with me then avoids me.

It daunts me and annoys me.

Ain't love grand?

Vulnerable

Be patient fearful heart.

Hold high your vision.

Make peace with yourself.

Let love guide you through

when no one can do,

what time most certainly will.

Put down your defenses and open your mind

to light and heal from within.

Then tell me you love me

I want to believe it.

I need you to show me.

But will you?

Bummer in the Summer

Lighten up!

Bring it up to the top and I'll be waiting there.

It's true that you've been holding out on me

and I can see you've got no time.

And baby I believe you've lost your mind.

It's always raining numbers

and it's always blowin' time.

Cutting into my days and into my nights.

Just shut the books and cut the lines.

If you don't think I'm right,

then baby I believe I'll lose my mind.

Cinderella

What ever made you run from me?

Did I scare you with my anger or my lust?

You know that I am here for you

and all I need is trust.

Don't say the words, don't make a move.

Don't turn and walk away

from me and mine and all we've spent,

cause baby there will come a day

that you will wonder

where I went?

And you will look, but you won't find

the girl who fits the shoe,

that hit your head beside the bed

while screaming "I love you!"

Thunder Road

I was hoping you could share

all the facets of what defines you to me.

But instead...

you chose to look away.

Too far away...

at something else that is an illusion.

I was hoping that you could see

from my side of the mirror

what you hold up for me to see.

There is no reflection of me...no love from you.

You show me pain in blown out proportions

of the simple needs this woman might have.

You bring me rain and you bring me thunder,

when all I need is warmth and understanding.

I'm only human.

Twisted

Why don't I love thee?

Let me count the whys

Lying

Deceiving

Conniving

Unfaithful

Obnoxious

Belligerent

Perverted

Raving freaking idiot

And those are your good points

Coming Undone

Honey dear one thing I ask

T'would make my joy forever last

This wish is just a wish for you

T'would make my dream of you come true

Picture this...

YOU

crawling on your hands and knees

five miles

uphill

on broken glass

under a blistering sun...

While I sit waiting…

naked and smiling...

fanning myself

in the shadow of a blooming lilac tree...

and drinking a cool and dirty Martini.

Don't hurry

I Only Cared for You

I don't care about the same things

you care about...

I only care for you.

I don't care to be a millionaire.

I only care for you..

You could have put the

business hell aside.

Let the money rollers all go by.

Drop the hookers and the bookies, for they all lie.

Put the movers and the shakers where they belong

which is nowhere near where I come from.

I don't care about the same things

you care about...

I only cared for you.

Somewhere down the Middle

Bring me the daylight.

Take back your night life.

Somewhere down the middle to find you and me.

Caught up in yesterday.

Still looking for a better way.

Somewhere down the middle to find you and me.

No bright lights no city nights.

No I'm sure it's not the life.

But I see things differently.

Dine me and dance me.

Yes you must romance me.

Somewhere down the middle to find you and me.

Take me home all alone.

Just you and me and a saxophone.

And somewhere down the middle

we'll find you and me.

No bright lights no city nights.

No I'm sure it's not the life.

But I see things differently.

Lights are On -- Nobody Home

Take the lampshade off of your head

Take your shoes out from under my bed.

Can't believe how little you've grown.

Lights are on but nobody's home.

And we're all hoping you're gonna get better,

but we all know you'll never be well

enough to walk the dog or mail a letter,

or hold this thing you call love together.

Better take that long walk NOW.

Call a cab or call a friend.

Catch my drift baby… this is the end.

Take your dish and your records too.

Can't believe I ever made it with you.

Mc Cloud

At Sebastian's we met.

You asked me to dance.

You bought me a drink.

I gave you my heart.

You were a sailor.

I was a stylist.

We spent the summer

flying on water.

You took my hand and took me south

in a red convertible under open skies.

Followed the coast down the 101

chasing the Washington Oregon

and California sun.

You told me you loved me.

That was your first mistake.

I believed you.

That was mine.

Hold

Wind blows and sand flies

up the alleys of my memories.

Looking thru it

I reach to it

How can I hold?

I've been here and I've been there.

I'd rather be here but when I'm not,

I'll paint it in my mind.

Remember it just as it is.

Perfect and poised.

Suspended in time.

A story untold

that never gets old.

How can I hold?

Deep Empty Blue

I woke last night to the sound of thunder.

Slipped from my bed to the cool night in wonder.

Looked far and wide to the deep empty sky.

Saw nothing but stars and moonlight

and knew why

there was no storm in the deep empty blue.

Only my heart

beating...

roaring..

wanting..

only you.

Compromise

My dreams are not far from where you say you are.

Into the night you come and you go.

I hear your voice… then it fades away.

And the moon has gone to another day.

And so I rise to compromise

for absent days

and quiet nights

with velvet dreams of you.

July Heat

Walk open eyed

thru the fire in my heart.

It burns ablaze...it calls your name.

In this tropical night

where are you?

Walk with me now

in the fires of desire.

Bring your sweet lips too close

to heaven and beyond.

Round and round

and slow and slow...

It won't be long now

when I'll turn to find you.

Will I find you?

Please be there.

Please

Pie in the Sky

Don't make the break, you know I'll wait.

The ship of fools is on its way.

Hear it coming.

Feel it nearing.

The tide is up and so are we.

Makes no difference how you slice it.

Pie in the sky for you and I.

Makes no difference how you slice it.

I got you and you got I.

Don't send no bills.

There'll be no dues,

for days of loss and nights abused.

Now is the time we've waited for.

Silver moonbeams on the shore.

Makes no difference how you slice it.

Pie in the sky for you and I.

Make no difference how you slice it.

I got you and you got I.

Port Augusta

Port Augusta beckons.

A beacon in the night.

The Powell River ferry

has shut its docks up tight.

So where do I stand to go now?

My dilemma plain in sight.

My Port Augusta beckons.

My beacon in the night.

Now when the skies start asking

for rain to chill my core,

I'll find my shelter from the storm

in this port along the shore.

That Day in Paris

Cracked porcelain skin…

glowing with graceful antiquity.

And those eyes…

What those sloping spheres have seen

I can't begin to imagine.

Hands petite…and skeletal

with thin lace gloves

blanketing their fragility.

On her lap…

a richly embroidered sachet

which whispers of former elegance

and haute couture.

And her lipstick

matches the invisible color of her rose parfum

that wafts and dances around her.

French-tinged English

massages

and teases my ears,

as she tells of a man

who swept her off her feet

in the cool summer rain

that pounded passionately

like cascading diamonds.

That day in Paris

Ambition

How the days drift on by.

Scarcely a whisper of wind.

Only time ... and you.

You the perfect one I hold high

on my list of joys

and sometimes sorrow.

Show me again how funny life can be

and how time can slip so far away.

Always the drive, the heat and the hunger.

Always the message

to seek and to follow.

Ambition...you are my hero.

Hungry for Steak

Hey you with the vibrating eyes

and the hand that paints God's will.

Where did you come from

and where are you going?

Do you hear what I'm asking you still?

Umbers and okras

on these you will dine.

Painting a world so different from mine.

I'm hungry for steak and you're hungry for oils.

Sometimes it simply makes my blood boil.

I'm fed up with you.

Finished with trying.

Better leave now while the paint is still drying.

Love in Vain

The rivers leading to and leaving from my heart
have all gone dry.
The effort and caring seem to all
have been in vain.

The wall is up…the chains around my heart
are locked and sealed.
I will never let you open them again.

You will never know the pain you have caused.
You are a thorn in my heart.

A Matter of Timing

Draw the line, anytime you want to.

Be my guest… take the rest

but just leave me one old song

to take me back to where I used to be.

Cause it's a matter of timing.

You know we both should be trying

to remain.

Ain't no use in pretending.

All this love we've been spending

should remain

just the same.

You've got your friends.

There's no end

but remember where I've been.

It's no sin to call yesterday

a better way.

Take me back to where I used to be.

Cause it's a matter of timing

You know we both should be trying

to remain.

Ain't no use in pretending.

All this love we've been spending

should remain

just the same.

Let Go

Overlooking the world

will come easier now.

Just a heartbeat that has gone to sleep

and a lifelong promise that you could not keep.

Let Go

Someday once more we will be happy.

I feel it in my heart.

We're only here for a moment of time

and now our ways must part.

Let Go

No tears from me, no love for you.

We've fallen off the course.

And now this torrid love affair

has ended in divorce.

Let Go

Back from Iraq

Give me time to heal the wound.

It's deep and you don't understand.

The place where I come from

has left me so undone.

And I don't know if I can recover.

My heart is heavy and my thoughts are veiled.

The mirror shows no reflection of me.

The words you are saying mean nothing at all

so please go away and leave me be.

Give me time to heal this wound.

It's deep and you don't understand.

The place where I come from

has left me so undone.

And I don't know if I can recover.

Via Del Norte

Bring to me
in golden mornings;
all your sweet love
from the cold night alone.

You can't know how warm
your love feels within me,
or how long the sun waits
for the moon to be gone.

The hours that slip between shadows of
darkness.
The heat that needs cooling from the fires
within.
The hours alone not having you near me..

It's all I can do to keep hanging on.

Battlefields 9/11

My love has not been here today.

Those scars remain on battlefields

in purple haze and violent sun

so deep inside an empty ruin

Where does he lie in quiet murmur?

Behind the walls ?

Before the Gods?

Breathing rage

through echoes of unforgiving

and praying softly for some chance of living.

Who will we cry for…

while we dance the lovers dance

and sing the sinners song.

Only to fall prey once more

to battlefields

in purple haze and violent sun

so deep inside an empty ruin.

My love has not been here today.

Cassandra

So much to ask from this fragile child.

Too much to take in a world that's gone wild.

Please stop the tears and stop the rain.

And Lord please take away her pain.

Bring her smile back to us now,

her sweet and sassy ways.

I ask you Lord to show me how

to brighten up her days.

Stay near her Lord for she is weak

and her struggle is never-ending.

Whisper to her as you speak

of love that you are sending.

With prayers and promise and hope and faith,

I know one day she'll find

some peace, an end to suffering,

in the healing arms of time.

Daughter at the Door

Don't forget to remember

when you're all torn up inside

and laid out in shreds like broken glass,

that beneath the mis-conceptions

he has of love,

only Truth is real.

And you know the Truth.

And that is your only consolation.

I've made mistakes

the same as you.

Only difference is

I needed someone

who understood

and loved me enough

to let me fall .

Thank you for falling...at my door.

Death of a Dog

Shining bright,

all that midnight light,

from the falling stars in your eyes of truth.

Tell me all the secrets in your heart

and if you ever leave me...

leave me easy.

Don't be long....Dream along...

I am here with you,

crying tears for you,

with a love that never

will not ever

die.

Do you know? Do you care?

If I close my eyes will you still be there?

Breathing

in the darkness... in the light.

All my deepest thoughts

are always there with you.

For I have never ever felt a love like this.

Just a passing moment of time with you.

And I will never ever hold the likes of you again.

All my deepest thoughts are

always there with you.

Go away Closer

Where were you when I needed you?
I'm just a child with a heart open wide
to the love that you always manage to hide.

I looked for you but you looked away.
I needed you to come and stay
and be my mother the one I trust.
The one who tells me that I must
be good and kind and helpful too.
Where were you when I needed you?

They say the devil fools with the best laid plans.
And I know your plan did not include me.
For a woman who is so accountable,
why does your love elude me?

They say we choose our mother before we choose the womb.

I know now why I chose her.

The lessons she taught from the cradle to the tomb

were

how to go away closer.

Good-Bye Daddy

The time has come

I knew it would,

for sad good byes and tears I've cried.

Lest old acquaintance be forgot,

these tears are not for you.

I cry for all the love inside

I can no longer give to you.

Grand Mothers

A grand mother's love is

and always will be,

a gift sent from heaven meant only for me.

She stands watching over the course of my life.

She guides and protects me.

Her strength is my light.

She whispers her prayers most times thru the night,

that her child be kept safe from pain and from strife.

Her babe is her world, her pride, her sunshine.

She knows she is blessed, her joy is sublime.

When worry falls on her,

a child gone astray...

Her arms open wider

and tears pave her way.

She stands firm and strong.

She fiercely protects.

She teaches me kindness and truth and respect.

For all the love and time she has spent,

I thank God above for the angel He sent.

Heaven Knows

Who writes the story of a life?

Where it should begin and where it should end?

Who calls the cast of players into being?

Who knows what gives man the want to live or the will to die?

From birth, we learn to walk the path that is lit before us.

Always looking for that light to lead the way so that we may give...

and get ... and grow.

Sometimes that path is dimmed.

Dimmed with disappointment, in ourselves and in others.

Narrowed by our weakness and paved with regrets.

And though we try to keep the light of hope and faith
shining...

the darkness prevails.

Who dims that light on our path?

That light that leaves us in the shadows of fear,

and creeping slowly behind it....despair.

Who knows the pain that looms largest on the path in a
man's day to day?

Those demons that take hold and will not let go.

Heaven knows...

For heaven waits for everyone.

Those who weep, those who suffer, those who give and
those who take.

Those who pray and those who don't.

All of us...the good the bad the indifferent.

The lonely, the weak and the strong.

I believe that Heaven writes the story of a life.

And in the end, the only thing it asks is to love and forgive.

And that is "ALL" it asks.

For our dear friend we ask Heaven

to love him as he loved us …and to forgive him… as we all do.

Little Girl Lost

Learn to forgive, learn to forget.

Learn to abandon ideologies and disbeliefs.

They are the bane of our society.

Set sail for light. Set sail for love.

Look for the tower.

Climb it if you can, and when you can

let me know… don't let me go.

Me, the weak and lowly pagan

in that sad kaleidoscope of fractured light

you call the truth.

Let me remind you...

Let me unwind you...

back to innocence, acceptance

and familiar joys.

Because I know where you can go.

Your path is wide and lit

by those who came before.

While you search your soul

and spend your tears,

let there not be shadows

cast upon your fears.

I'll always love you … at any cost.

Right now you're just

my little girl lost.

Loving a Married Man

My head hurts with the echoes
of a door closed, a back that turns.
Not knowing how to say the words
to make you understand...
that time away from you is
one eternity to another.

Will you meet me in your dreams?
Will you hold me in the warmth of your breath
with arms and legs entangled?
And when you wake will I be there?
If only on your mind.

Do you know that you have me shaking
with the fear of never really having you.
I truly hope you're not just passing thru.

I want tomorrow with you.

Mama Rose

Please don't leave without saying good-bye.
I'll do my best to be strong and brave.
I'll bring love to your son and all of your babies
and do my best not to cry.

I know you're ready for a brighter tomorrow
the road's been long and you are tired.
The end is near this I know and
your time with us will soon expire.

I will remember all your smiles
and how you knew just what to say.
I know you can't promise me another day
but please don't leave without saying goodbye.

Wedding Night

The bride was young and virgin.

The groom was very nervous.

The guests had gone...

the time had come

for him to be courageous.

She slipped into another room

preparing for the consummation.

He paced the floor

staring at the door

and waited

for his moment of elation.

The door flew open and there she stood

in all her naked splendor.

In all his years he'd never felt

a love so pure and tender.

He offered to her his honor.

Obliging... she honored his offer.

And all night long

to the beat of song,

it was perpetual honor and offer.

Mister Man

How could I get any higher on you?

Call it by any other name you must

but I believe Mister Man

has done away with my all.

Like a bandit in the night

stealing only glimpses of himself

thru mirrors overhead

when he looks within my eyes.

The eyes you say?

I think it's more...

Much more

Suddenly Summer

How my soul was lifted
and wings sprung from my heart.
I soared above the seagulls cry
and could not tell us apart.

A smile was etched upon my face.
The ocean filled my eyes.
Staring into time and space
where mind and body lies.

Between the forest and the beach
we christened our lust and hunger.
I have a song within my reach
I call it "suddenly summer"

In that moment of wild abandon,
I know I've left a memory.
A song that echoes in the canyon
and a heart carved on a tree.

No Agenda

Music wafts all around…

…caressing like a breeze.

A distant flutter of wings…it seems

the winds are whispering to the trees.

Caught for a spell between the sea the sand

and the stars.

No prayers, no promises, no lies

no wars.

Only a smiling heart and ocean eyes

A love so grand...

A life fulfilled...

A day with no agenda.

This Man of Mine

Please don't wake this man of mine.

The spell he's under...a dream sublime.

Love came knocking and to my surprise

it only took one look in his eyes.

He mustn't wake for I fear he'll find

it's only a dream … a space in time.

Only in his arms, his lips to mine.

Behind his eyes, beyond his dreams.

I live for him, love only him.

He cannot know what this moment means.

So please don't wake this man of mine.

Tahiti

Warm sleepy mornings waking next to you;

nothing on earth has ever felt better.

I had a dream, a wonderful dream

and it just goes on and on.

Taking me...holding me

with a love that never ends.

There's not a lot of change in my life

but I do know this..

How can I ever let you go?

Antonio

If I told you just how I felt.

If I told you that you were the one

that softens my heart

and warms like the sun.

Would you stay Antonio?

Would you stay?

If you told me that I was something special.

If you told me that this time it's real;

it would take from me all of the doubt

that clouds my mind

and I would shout

to the heavens above

"Here is Love"

"Here is Love"

If I told you just how I felt.

If I told you that you were the one.

Would you stay Antonio?

Would you stay?

Sweet Lorraine

Look at me...look in me.

Who do you see?

What do you feel?

Close your eyes and smile

I am there...

Do you see me?

I'm the one who waits while darkness falls.

Watching for your step…

Waiting for your call…

In between your silence

where you have built your wall.

You can't know how many times I have

glanced across tables

gazed across rooms

and stared across oceans;

hoping to find you my sweet Lorraine

looking at me … looking in me ….

with eyes wide open and smiling

into all of my tomorrows.

Winter Grief – Spring Relief

Wasn't it only yesterday my dear?
All wrapped up in winters dread,
we sat around the fireplace
in wait of summer days ahead.

The lonely weeks, the sadness there,
the grief, the sorrow we did share.
The wind and rain how cold it blew
when it would end no one knew.

And then the miracle arrived
that took us from the winters edge.
Out from 'neath a sea of cold
into a sun of gleaming gold.

You took my hand and led me down
to where the ocean meets the sand
and there you made my dreams come true.
Spring, I've been waiting just for you.

Was it you?

Or the salt-sweet air

that kissed my body lying there...

Between the sand and sea I fell...

How long...? How far...?

I could not tell.

The Seed

Every trial, every failure

and every heartache

carries along with it

the **seed** of a greater day.

Waiting for its time to come around

and sprout and bloom.

So

rise everyday with a smile

on your face

and wander in your sunshine day.

And though there may be a darkened hour,

have faith… there is a greater power

in the **seed** that has the patience

to become a flower.

Casa Antomar

Hey gringo I'm talkin' to you!

I can see what you're tryin' to do.

Building a castle in a foreign land

with views of the ocean and beaches of sand.

I admire your pride in this undertaking, but you're

gonna go crazy while this home you are making.

It may take you longer than you had expected

but it will be worth it when this home is erected.

Make a wish upon a star

and call this Casa Antomar.

Cause when it's all been said and done

ridin' high, feelin' number one...

There will be no mountain that you can't climb.

The sky will open.

Your sun will shine.

Daughter with a Diamond

If I have but one chance to tell you

of the doubt I feel inside;

then now is the time I must disclose

my thoughts about this man you chose.

My little one, my little one...

Make choices wise with heart and mind

and eyes wide open too.

Your gift is time

to think it through

with grace...with God...

and my love for you.

Choose well,

remembering always in your dreams

what the promise of "I DO" really means.

Lilli Bird

Lilli bird my darling sweet

at just one minute old…

you stole my heart.

You

with your tuft of poker hair and cupid lips

and eyes as black as night.

I am overflowing with joy

at such a beautiful sight.

The angels must have been happy

the night they dreamed of you.

Please always be good to your namma.

Her love for you is true.

Grand-Children

Put your shells in an empty bucket

and save them all for me.

You never know when the time will come

the place will be

you'll look and see...

Was it you?

Was it me?

who saved the shells along the shore

and tucked their dreams along the shelf.

We'll laugh to find that what we saved

is waiting there

in that time and place.

We'll look and see..

It was you

It was me

who saved the shells along the shore

and tucked their dreams along the shelf.

Liam Daniel

My heart is filled with sunshine
and beauty.
Today I have my first grand-son
And boy is he a cutie!

He is fair and sweet and
the prince I have waited for.
Thank you to all the angels in the room
I saw you standing at the door.

Serves You Right

Meet me down by the railway station.

I've been waiting...

Anticipating...

Chasing that same damn fool.

Well you know that I don't mind,

but sometimes it seems that I

trusted

and trusting is crazy

and crazy is to wait on YOU baby.

So please,

I've been taking my time

and you know you've been on my mind.

I hope you find love.

Your own designs of love.

One that serves you right

One that serves you right

I believe yes,

I believe that I know you.

But till you walk thru my eyes I'll never show you

that I hold the secret of your darkest night,

and its shadow

lies waiting in my morning light.

So please,

I've been taking my time

and you know you've been on my mind.

I hope you find love.

Your own designs of love.

One that serves you right

One that serves you right

A Better Way

You're a frantic frightened businessman

that I can't bring myself to understand,

when the answers to your questions are all in your hand.

We're caught up in the madness and the hurry just to win
the race.

I need to know that when I'm lost I'll turn around and see
His face.

Take that call ...do it all..

Losin' time...chasin' dimes.

Can't we stop and slow it to a crawl?

Listen to Him now,

for we all must learn how

to hear what He is trying to say

and thank the Lord for another day.

He knows that there's a better way.

The Main Ingredient

I often think of my house as my soul.

The place where I find quiet and comfort.

And every room of this palace does hold

the love of my labor and effort.

A sanctuary from daybreak to dark,

a safe haven I call my own.

But my kitchen is the room that holds my heart

and makes this house a home.

If walls could talk,

my kitchen would tell

of years when time was lenient...

When supper time was family time

and love was the main ingredient.

Write it Down

Expression does not wait to be born.

It will find you and fill you and then forget you.

So write it down

Expression takes no prisoners.

It has no fear or shame.

Expression will seduce you

and then it will reduce you

to an ember that has no flame.

So write it down

Expression comes disguised as reverie

…a flash of light so bright in the distance...

sparking something in your memory.

Grasp the moment at every instance

before it becomes too dark to see.

So write it down

Expression is not my friend.

Nor is it my enemy.

Not really a poet or a preacher,

but expression is my teacher.

And so I write it down.

Swimming Lessons

So much water must flow

under the bridge of perseverance.

Current masked as love

and undertow as affection.

Thinking you may drown

in confusion and rejection.

Eventually we wade out of the water,

with the beauty of a white winged dove.

And build a stronger safer place

for our selves

and those we love.

Intuition

In every rose garden

there is one flower that stands high above the rest.

One that watches over all the others.

Loving them into their fullest

and pointing them toward their best.

She is the pillar of the garden.

The one that is proud of all the others.

The strongest to weather the wind and rain.

The first to share the suns early rays

and the last to bid the moon goodnight.

In my garden that rose has a name

and her name is "Intuition"

Intuition watches over me with the grace and the patience
of an angel.

She cares for me deeply.

She loves me unconditionally

and she lights the path before me.

She is my sister…my confidante….my mentor …and my
closest friend.

The depth of my gratitude for her guidance and counsel

can never be expressed.

The words that intuition whispers to me

are kind when I am distressed.

My faith in the world today

would never have been as strong,

if Intuition had not been there

to guide and push me along.

Seeds of Hope

The choices we make today are but a glimpse

into the choices we make tomorrow.

Though the past be gone

it's mark has been replaced.

There is now a furrow in its place.

A space to sow the seeds of hope

and the grains of wisdom too.

A place to wake to each sunrise

and a place to depend on what we know

to be just and right and true.

Have we forgotten or simply overlooked

that this is God's green earth.

Our gift, our heritage on loan for today.

HE promised.

Everything we need is everything we have.

Offered up to us ready for the reception

in a splendor so blindingly beautiful

that it may cause our eyes to close

and our souls to fall asleep…

Masterpiece

From the deep swell of tranquility,

warmed by dappled sunlight,

sketched in the wind of soft fragility,

a masterpiece was in sight.

Its colors were not from this world.

Its strokes were from some other time and space.

And it spoke to me

of some far away place,

where losing yourself meant finding yourself

but never leaving a trace.

It wrapped me up and held me out

in the warmth of crimson and teal.

Out from a sky so deep in blue

to a burning sun that I could feel.

When all the vivid spirited colors

were there for me to see,

the masterpiece was whispering

that

you're in love with me.

Millennium

Welcome year 2000.

You've been hiding round the corner for so long.

Now you arrive in a bright sunrise

with the chirp of a robins song.

You hold the promise of a beautiful century

filled with hope and change and dreams to come true.

Hold my loved ones near to me.

Keep us humble and faithful too.

Deal me the perfect hand.

I'll play my cards the best I can.

God is Big

There is a pot of gold at the end of the rainbow.

We must believe it to see it.

You and I and the world.

For as we continue to reach for

the definition of love and life,

perhaps today we're one smile closer.

Nothing is too good to be true.

Nothing is too good to last.

Nothing is too wonderful to happen.

God is big...

Life is wonderful...

and we are so richly blessed.

Sara Lee and Herbal Tea

Got to join the race to find a place.

A house, a home, a family.

Some Sara Lee and Herbal Tea

to ease the day's un-wind.

A Jenny shake, banana cake

and cookies on the counter.

A hearth of stone at Christmas time

with stockings hung together.

Along the race we find a place

to watch the days unwind.

Some Sara Lee and Herbal tea

to leave it all behind.

The moon is up, the sun is not.

What can you call your own these days?

Besides the stars there's little else

that doesn't fall away.

Epiphany

Bring to me your sadness
and I will bring you hope.
When all the skies are darkened
only then you'll know.

The light in your eye shows.
The whisper in your heart knows
that Love is the answer
we're all looking for.

It will bring you gladness
and peace forever more.
When you find that Love is the answer
you will look no more.

Stand in His light

and feel your power grow.

Take the strength

that heaven's God sent,

wherever you may go.

Forgiveness

You don't deserve to be hurt this way

by a son to whom you gave

your love, your trust … your wisdom, your all.

You paved the way

for him to stand tall.

One day he'll see the wrong he's done.

The pain he's caused…the love he's lost.

I wonder if he ever thinks of this

or what his pride has cost.

As long as he refuses to see

that honor is what he lacks,

then wasted time is stolen time.

Something he can never give back.

I know your heart is breaking

and the hole is as big as the sky.

Forgiveness is not an easy task

but please say you'll give it a try.

Love Light

Gone forever

are the days when the sun would not shine

and the blackened nights would find me

on my knees…

praying for the light I need.

Gone forever

are the shadows in the dark

and the saddened lonely heart

cause you give me all the love I need.

Your sun brightens up my day.

Your moon lights up my night.

It's good to have you give me

all the light I need.

Thank you for your love,

Jesus

Thank you for your light

in my desperate time of need.

Finding Forever

Out of the night an angel came to me.

Her hands held out to mine.

Her voice like music…softer than the rain

Clothed in crinoline, she whispered my name.

I gazed into her eyes and saw a million stars.

I touched her hand

and knew I held the hand of God.

Come with me she said.

I've been waiting for so long…

to take you up..

to take you in..

to take you home.

But how will I go I asked.

You'll sail on the wind and ride on the stars.

And what will I see?

The rays of the sun and the glow of the moon.

And what will I hear?

The cry of a newborn and the song of the sea.

And what will I feel?

The warmth of the sun and the depth of my love.

And what will I find?

She answered ...

"My beloved...you will find me

... and you will find forever."

Mother in the Mirror

I met you today in the silence of my memory.

Your smile and your eyes reminded me of rain.

A dim and quiet veil upon your face

spoke to me of distant pain.

We said all that we had to say

though we didn't speak a word.

The sweetest sounds came from your heart

that I have ever heard.

In silence we both held our tongue

and thoughts crossed from each other.

I'm looking in the mirror now

and I can see my mother.

I think I know now what you meant

when you said" Wait and see.

If you should miss me,

you can find me

in the silence of your memory."

Grace

A photograph.

An epitaph.

A song and a sweet memory.

An old photo binder....a kind reminder

of the beauty that once followed me.

The smile that lay upon my lips.

The color that flushed my cheeks.

Where have you gone sweet mother of time?

Ninety years seems only like weeks.

The years that we spend

thinking there is no end,

for we all must keep up the pace.

With courage and pride

there by our side;

the most we can ask for

is Grace.

To Thank You

Where would I be without family?

To help me and lift me when I need a boost.

Though I have traveled far and wide

this bird has always

come home to roost.

So very young when I left the nest.

When life was calling and time was endless

and each new day was sacred and blessed.

They watched my parade of escapades.

Their patience I certainly put to the test !

My family stood by me

and watched me fly,

with a smile on their face

and a tear in their eye.

Learning my lessons

through error and sin,

that sometimes you lose

and sometimes you win.

I would not be who I am today

it's true,

if it were not for the love

I got from you.

These words are written

to say "thank you"

Marion Kremer

About the Author

Marion has been writing since the age of 13. She was born in Alberta Canada and raised her 2 daughters on Vancouver Island, Hawaii and Palm Springs. She enjoys music, photography, cooking, travel, and writing. Speaks 3 languages and plays piano, guitar and percussion. Her husband Anthony (Tony) is an accomplished artist. They live in Southern California and Baja Mexico.